# Number 3:
# The God Number

# Number 3:
# The God Number

Jeffrey L. Garman

| Library of Congress Control Number: | | 2010908590 |
| --- | --- | --- |
| ISBN: | Hardcover | 978-1-4535-2064-2 |
| | Softcover | 978-1-4535-2063-5 |
| | Ebook | 978-1-4535-2065-9 |

This book was printed in the United States of America.

**To order additional copies of this book, contact:**
Xlibris Corporation
1-888-795-4274
www.Xlibris.com
Orders@Xlibris.com
82180

# CONTENTS

Chapter 1: Origin of Number 3........................................ 13

Chapter 2: The Characteristics of God ........................... 17

Chapter 3: Time ............................................................ 21

Chapter 4: Creation....................................................... 27

Chapter 5: The Flood..................................................... 31

Chapter 6: Abraham....................................................... 37

Chapter 7: Jesus Christ: Birth and Childhood ............... 45

Chapter 8: Ministry........................................................ 49

Chapter 9: Crucifixion and Resurrection........................ 56

Chapter 10: More Things about Number 3..................... 60

Chapter 11: Conclusion.................................................. 63

# DEDICATION

I would like to dedicate this book to my faithful wife Marcy and my two outstanding children Ashley and Daniel. Also, I like to dedicate this to my Lord Jesus Christ for what He did for me that day on the cross of Calvary.

# ACKNOWLEDGEMENT

I would like to thank Charles Wasilefski and his associate Stephen Moore for encouraging me to have started with this work. I also want to thank a dear friend Rick Kauffman for motivating me to keep on going.

I also want to thank some of Xlibris' Publishing staff; Kathy Santos, Shannon Tyler, and Marian Lumayag for their wonderful work with me. These girls deserve a five-star rating! These three are angels! Thank you.

A powerful, in-depth look at God, to help us see what and who our God really is . . .
And where we are in history, through Biblical numbers . . .

—Jeffrey Garman

In everyone's life, ever since Adam, it seems we all live it in a great forest, and the forest is made up of our everyday experiences—our successes, heartaches, appetites, needs, culture, family, friends, and experiences of our lives. These are the trees in the forest that we live in. We spend our lifetimes working among these trees in this great forest, and for most folks, there are only a few, and every person's group of trees is different. Some are in totally different areas of this great forest and in different ages and cultures. However, they are all in, and live their lives in, this same ancient forest. We all live and die here, but there is so much more . . . If only we could rise above the trees and see the whole forest, or maybe just a glimpse of the big picture, if only for a little while, we could understand ourselves and our world a little bit better than we did before. That is my purpose here, to show you more about God and humanity . . . and how God is the creator of the great forest and all peoples of all times . . . He is also the creator of our numbers and 3 is the greatest number—THE GOD NUMBER.

# CHAPTER 1

## Origin of Number 3

God is a trinity or a triune being. He is the Father, the Son, and the Holy Spirit. The Creator is 3 individual spirit beings that act and make decisions in total agreement. They are 3 as one. All things that were made were made by him and through him. The universe and all that is in it was created by God *The Almighty*, **the Trinity**, the 3 as one.

The name **Jehovah, YHWH,** means *the God that is*, present tense; *the God that was*, past tense; *the God that is to come*, future tense. God is the creator of time itself. When God spoke to Moses at the burning bush, he described himself this way: "*I am the God of Abraham, I am the God of Isaac, and I am the God of Jacob*" (Exod. 3:6). When Moses asked God who he should say sent him, when he addressed his people, God said to him, "**I AM, THAT I AM.**" Maybe he was saying to Moses, "I am the God that was, I am the God that is, and I am the God that is to come." **I AM, THAT I AM**. I am the God of everything! From the beginning to end.

Do you see how God describes himself? In 3's. Is it because he is a triune being? When Jesus was in his earthly ministry, he also spoke of himself as **I AM.** Jesus said, "*I am the way, I am the truth, and I am the life, no man comes to the father but by me . . .*" (John 14:6). Notice again how he describes himself: in 3 ways. Then notice what he says: There is no way to God, but by me, and what I am going to do, on the cross of Calvary. Only by believing that Jesus Christ died on that Roman cross almost two thousand years ago, shedding his blood for our sins, is there any access to God at all. Don't let anyone fool you into thinking there are many ways to God; there are not! Christ made that perfectly clear by his statement . . . Don't be deceived by a preacher who leads you to believe that if you go to church and put money in the offering plate, or if you are religious or do religious things that is all it takes, or if you are a good person, you are then, OK with God . . . Jesus says: **NO!** Except you come through me, you don't come at all. Jesus said, *"I am the way."* I am the way to eternal life. I am the only way for mankind. *"I am the truth."* God is all truth. Satan is the father of lies and deception. His deceptions are everywhere, fogging our conceptions of God, twisting, distorting, and perverting everything we know about the Almighty. Jesus also said, *"I am the life,"* He is the life and light of mankind. He is the one that breathed life into Adam. He is the life giver. This God that breathed life into humanity and created the cosmos is the same God that hung on that Roman cross and died there. He humbled himself and became as weak human being on this planet called Earth to suffer and die for us and then to rise from the dead on the 3rd day. He that never knew sin, the Ageless One, who never knew death, willingly died here. Wow! What a story! It is the greatest love story ever told.

Another name for God is **El Shad-dai,** *the all-sufficient one.* The Trinity has need of nothing or no one. But it seems to me that God loves to create wonderful things that are perfect and wholesome. You can see that on a beautiful spring day when the flowers and the trees are in bloom and everything is green. It is awesome to see and smell. Clear sparkling water so pure you can dip your cup into the cold running water and be so satisfied, birds singing songs to God, clean, crisp air so easy to breathe, beautiful mountains, canyons, and glaciers—all created for the glory of God. And that brings us to the second characteristic of El

Shad-dai, God the Almighty. The Almighty rules the universe and everything in it. When I look at my computer monitor at pictures from the Hubble Telescope, it is stunning to see how much is in our universe and the vast distance between everything. How great is our God! The 3rd part of El Shad-dai is *God of the Mountain.* Whenever I look at a great mountain, I think of God. God of the Mountains. When God gave Moses the Ten Commandments, it was on a mountain—The Mount Sinai.

**ADONAI,** another name for God, means *LORD*. God is not only our Lord but our father—our heavenly Father—and we can come to him with our needs and our joys. He is our Master, the helper of our daily lives. He is our teacher, helping us to mature into the likeness of his dear son. He wants us to grow up and be fruitful in our lives, honoring him with our actions and decisions. He loves our praise and worship, godly worship that honors him. I can't for the life of me see how most of the contemporary Christian music honors God. It is tasteless to say the least. It sounds like the ungodly music of our wicked, immoral culture. How foolish to think that this trash honors God at all. Wholesome music can be broken down to 3 parts: rhythm, melody, and harmony, in singing the lyrics. When these 3 are played and sung in a correct balance, it is beautiful. When you listen to beautiful godly music like this, it brings tears to your eyes. It is almost like listening to the breath of God. But this trashiness I hear from many churches today, called contemporary worship, is nothing but a deception of the devil, to me. I saw a praise and worship service on TV several years ago, and the worship leader, the leader of the rock band, was leading with his guitar. He was covered with huge tattoos all over his exposed arms and neck. They were singing rap, and these were the lyrics: "Send down the power, Send down the rain." This was chanted over and over for about twenty minutes. As a matter of fact, he didn't even play that guitar but just was swinging it around and pounding on it. If there was a pianist in that rock band, he just pounded on the same note the entire time. That auditorium was packed with youth, and they were waving their arms and dancing.

God is the creator of music, and I can tell you he did not create that! I can only imagine what worship will be like in heaven . . . Glorious singing to the Lamb that was Slain . . . I can almost in my mind's ear hear it now:

> *Redeemed how I love to proclaim it, Redeemed by the blood of the Lamb,*
> *Redeemed through his infinite mercy, His child and forever I am,*
> Redeemed, redeemed, redeemed by the blood of the Lamb,
> *His child and forever I am . . .*

Years ago I attended several seminars; I remember singing that glorious hymn in harmony with four or five thousand people in those great auditoriums, and you cried and sang. It was beautiful beyond words. We sang to our King, our Sovereign, and this is another part of the name **ADONIA**. He is the **King of Kings** and **Lord of Lords**, and Lord, we worship you . . .

# CHAPTER 2

## The Characteristics of God

God is **omniscient,** *THE ALL-KNOWING GOD.* He knows the beginning and the end of everything. Jesus Christ said, "I am the *ALPHA* and the *OMEGA,* **the beginning and the end.**" Those are the first and last letters of the Greek alphabet. God understands everything, even time itself. It seems to me that he is the beginning and the end of everything in present tense. What a concept that is! That is how he knows the future. And this is why Christ describes himself as *I AM.* He knows every star, every planet, every galaxy, every moon. He knows it in present tense. From creation to its end. Every angel, every heavenly being he ever created. He knows every human being that was ever born or will be born. He knows every hair on the head of each person that was ever born. I also believe he knows our genetics to the last detail. He knows every action and the total intent of our hearts. Every baby that was or will be aborted he knows intimately. I think God is more concerned about the condition of our selfish, flesh-loving hearts than how totally sexy we are, don't you think? Do you think we have an epidemic of lust-laden, immoral perversion here? I don't think it takes a genius to see that. I met a pretty lady about a year ago at the grocery store who was working at the deli, and we struck up a conversation about the Lord. I talk about the Lord almost everywhere I go. I asked her if she was born-again, and she told me she certainly was, and then she informed me that she attended this huge mainline Bible-teaching church in our area that I will not name. She said that she and her boyfriend pray together every night before going to bed. I almost fell down when she said that, but I stayed composed and asked another relatively pointed question: "It must be difficult to do that and then drive home every night?" "Oh no," she said, "we live together. We pray before we go to bed." This lady was serious and looked, to me, to be in her early forties. And this is what she must have thought being born-again was like. Now wouldn't you think a Bible-teaching church would have taught them better than that—that you cannot live in sexual immorality and expect an inheritance with God? Sexual immorality is sin! (Gal. 5:19-21)

God knows the future as well as the past and present. That is why there is so much emphasis on prophecy. There are 33 prophecies about Jesus Christ in the Old Testament. All of these proved to be correct, and they were all written hundreds and even a thousand or more years before he was even born. They were detailed prophecies about his life and death and Second Coming. Would you please take note of how many there are? **33.**

God is **omnipotent,** *THE ALL-POWERFUL ONE.* God can do whatever he wants in his universe. But God will not act against his nature. He does not sin. Neither can he ignore sin. He must deal with it in his way, but he also forgives sin. He deals with the Sin of Lucifer, who was the one that brought sin and rebellion to the cosmos. God is dealing with him in his way. He has a divine plan, and we are part of it! But *"God's ways are not our ways. God's ways are above our ways as far as the heavens are from the earth.* The Lord is righteous in all of his ways and holy in all of his works"* (Ps. 145:17). There will be a time again when there will be no sin in the universe, but not yet. However, it seems to me that we are almost at the Rapture and our days of dealing with this sinful world will be over, and I am ready! Even so come Lord Jesus!

God is **omnipresent,** *THE ONE THAT IS EVERYWHERE AT ALL TIMES.* No other beings have these attributes or powers, only God. Satan does not have the abilities of God at all. His knowledge of us and all of mankind comes from his immeasurable age and his vast network of evil fallen angels and demons. Satan can only be at one place at a time. But he has an entire spirit army of wicked beings feeding him with information about us. They want to destroy us at any moment here on planet Earth. These wicked fallen angels hate us. They have hated us all the way back to Adam! Satan and his army of devils hate every human being that was ever born. Their hatred is an all-consuming fire. But why? Is it because God so loves his creation of humanity on this little planet called Earth in the far away Milky Way Galaxy? Yes, I think so . . . absolutely so . . . But the devil and his armies of devils want to drag humanity to hell right along with them! His plan is to deceive every human, and I believe these fallen beings are giddy with glee every time a person dies in sin and alienation from God, because they know how much it hurts the Almighty. God did not create the Lake of Fire for us but for the devil and his angels, and it is another notch in the enemy's belt every time another sinner ends his or her life in an eternal hell that was not made for them even after God provided an escape for us. The devil knows where he is going, and pardon the expression, is "mad as hell," to put it mildly. But there will come a day, I believe, after Satan and his legions of devils have been cast into the lake of fire forever and after God cleanses the cosmos of their rebellion and sin, when God the Almighty will address them all, especially the devil, and maybe say something like this, "You rebelled against me after I created you with everything. You had eternal life, freedom, beauty, power, the wisdom and brilliance of the ages. You were The Morningstar, the greatest being ever created and you had everything any being could have ever WANTED, and you rebelled and brought SIN into a sinless universe . . . But I have children on that little planet, Earth, who have sincerely loved me and loved my Son even though many had horrible, wretched lives. Many even gave almost everything for me, some even their very health and lives! You did every form of evil to them, every form of deception, but I kept them, and by faith, they clung to me and the cross. They never saw or knew what you know. They had nothing and were nothing compared to you, but yet they believed and obeyed me, and I was their God. And by that testimony, you know that I am just in what I have done to you." However, all of these ideas are my thoughts; keep that in mind. Let God be truth, and every man be a liar. There is no divine inspiration here in my reasoning. The Word of God is truth.

# CHAPTER 3

## Time

God is also the creator of time itself. God's time is not like our time. There is no day or night or Monday or Tuesday in heaven. There are no three-day weekends in heaven. No holidays. There are no seasons there, no months like June or July or any month at all. There are no years or decades or even centuries there. I am not trying to appear stupid here or belay this point. I am just trying to help you to grasp this concept in your mind, for time in heaven, where God's throne is, is totally different than anything we have ever known. God created our time for us. Our time has to do with our own planet Earth. All of humanity experiences time in the same universal way. Here on earth we have a 7-day week. God created the earth and mankind in 6 days, and on the 7th day he rested. He was so tired! Now there is a new concept: A tired God . . . No, I don't think God gets tired as we do. He did that for us! He created Adam on the 6th day, thus making number 6 the number of man. Also, he made number 7 the number of completion with God.

I have heard preachers say for almost fifty years that 7 is the number of God, but that is incorrect. The number 3 is the number of God, and 7 is the number of completeness or being finished.

Now back to where we were . . . There are 60 seconds in a minute. There is a number 6 in that, for humanity. There are 60 minutes in one hour, another 6 for humanity. There are 12 hours in one revolution of the clock, or ½ of a 24-hour day. The number 12 is another number of God. There were 12 disciples, 12 tribes of Judah, 12 gates to the coming New Jerusalem, the Holy City of God. The number 24 is another number, but this number is for resurrected born-again believers, in heaven, seated around the throne of the Almighty, wearing white robes and crowns.

> And round about the throne were four and twenty seats: and upon the seats I saw four and twenty elders sitting, clothed in white raiment; and they had on their heads crowns of gold (Rev. 4:4). The four and twenty elders fall down before him that sat on the throne, and worship him that liveth for ever and ever, and cast their crowns before the throne, saying, Thou art worthy, O Lord, to receive glory and honor and power: for thou hast created all things, and for thy pleasure they are and were created. (Rev.4:10)

Doesn't that give you goose bumps? It certainly does to me! There are 12 months in a year. There are 365 days in a year. Here number 3 is for God, and 6 is for humanity. It is the number of days it takes the Earth to make a complete revolution around the Sun in its orbit. I understand the ancient Hebrew calendar had 360 days in it, compared with ours now. But the point is still the same. We are the 3rd planet from the sun. 3, again. If I remember correctly from school, the Earth is 93 million miles from the Sun. Adam, the Bible says, was 930 years old when he died. Maybe there is a connection . . . Now I have discussed these biblical numbers with you to show you another footprint of God. These numbers seem, to me, to give us proof of God from an entirely different source.

I will give you another illustration about time, which may explain even clearer the difference between our time and God's time. Imagine that you and your wife are space travelers. You have this incredibly large, fast space ship. It has a food and water generation system that will last forever. You have unlimited oxygen or air, but you have traveled five thousand light years from Earth and you ran out of gas. The engines won't restart. Now you are stuck somewhere in deep space forever. You won't get too lonely, for you have your sweetheart with you. But here is the problem. After you are in that space ship for a very long time, will you continue to see time as you did back home? Maybe, for a little while, you will count what you think is a day or a week or a month and a year, but everything is the same; every moment in your ship is locked in space. Time as you know it will stop. Every moment will be the same forever! You will eat and sleep, do exercises, play your favorite games, but it will always be that same day, forever. That is the way it is, it seems to me, to be with God in heaven. There will be no night or seasons or climate changes or anything like we have now. There will be no need of the sun, for God will be the light. I remember reading, when I was a boy, a sign in a church that said, "*Jesus Christ, the Same, Yesterday, Today and Forever,*" that is what that means . . . No one will complain that it is too hot or too cold. There is no aging, no dying, no sickness, no hospitals, no homes for old folks, no children starving to death, no more changing of clothes, for they will never get dirty or ever wear out. No more shaving, thank God! There is no changing in heaven. "*I am the Lord your God, I change not.*" Maybe it is like a day that never ends . . . In our heavenly bodies I am sure we can travel anywhere we want to just by thinking about it, but we will not be the same as now. Nothing except our love for our Lord will be the same. Time as we know it now will have totally ended forever when we get over there.

As we have been talking about time, let us move back again to our time here on planet Earth. 2 Peter 3:8 says something very informative and different about our Earth time. Peter makes a comparison, and it seems to me that it was written to help us understand better the Second Coming of Jesus Christ. This is what it says: "But beloved be not ignorant of this one thing, that one day is as a thousand years, and a thousand years as one day." One day with God is compared to one thousand years to humanity. Just following this, Peter says this:

> But the day of the Lord will come as a thief in the night; in which the heavens will pass away with a great noise, and the elements shall melt with fervent heat, the Earth also and the works that are therein shall be burned up. (Verse 10)

> Seeing that all these things shall be dissolved, what manner of persons ought you to be in all holy living and godliness. (Verse 11)

> Looking for and hasting unto the coming of the day of God, wherein the heavens being on fire shall be dissolved and the elements shall melt with fervent heat. (Verse 12)

Here we see the context in which Peter was speaking, the Second Coming of Christ. God created the earth in 6 days, and now the comparison has been made to 6 *thousand years of humanity*. But everyone knows that the earth as we now know it is older than 6 thousand years, everyone! But what you may not realize is, God created everything with age. Adam was not a one-day-old baby when he was created, but a full grown adult. The same for Eve. The trees, the animals, the mountains, the oceans, and everything in them were created with age, some with great age. The trees in the Garden of Eden bore fruit. It takes adult trees to bear fruit.

Now, many Bible historians believe that we have passed the 6-thousand-year mark in the history of humanity and are now in a transition time to the millennial reign of Jesus Christ—the one-thousand-year reign of Christ on the earth, as compared to the 7th day of creation, keeping in mind again that Peter says *one day is as a thousand years*. This millennial reign will be a reign without the influence of the devil and his fallen angels or demons. Satan will be chained then and cast into the bottomless pit for one thousand years (Rev. 20:1-3). The Antichrist and the False Prophet will be cast alive into the lake of fire. And the remnant of humanity and devils that fought against the Lord (Rev. 19:20-21; Matt. 25:41). However, we have a problem! For between the Church Age, or the Age of Grace that we are in now, and the one-thousand-year reign of Christ is the 7-year tribulation period in which the Antichrist will rule the earth. His number will be 666, the number of man repeated 3 times. This is a representation of a man trying to be God. Remembering that the number of God is 3, the repetition of 6 three times emulates this number. A further mock of God is the false trinity: 3 evil beings mimicking God. This trinity consists of Satan, the Antichrist, and the false prophet. These 3 will lead mankind into a great war against God. This will be the second war Satan leads against God. The first war was in heaven. He was defeated and ⅓ of the angels that fought with him were cast out. And it seems that we are standing right in front of that 7-year tribulation period, which will lead to that second war, The Battle of Armageddon. But Satan will wage a 3rd war against God at the end of the one-thousand-year millennial reign of Jesus Christ. After the 7-year tribulation period and the Battle of Armageddon where Satan and his legions are defeated, he will be cast and chained in the bottomless pit for a thousand years (Rev. 20:1-3).

> And I saw an angel come down from heaven, having the key to the bottomless pit and a great chain in his hand. And he laid hold of the dragon the old serpent, which is the Devil and Satan, and bound him one thousand years. And cast him into the bottomless pit, and shut him up, and set a seal upon him, that he should deceive the nations no more, till the thousand years should be fulfilled; and after that, he must be loosed a little season. (Rev. 20:7-10)

> And when the thousand years are expired, Satan shall be loosed out of his prison, and shall go out to deceive

the nations which are in the four quarters of the earth, Gog and Magog, to gather them together to battle: the number of whom is as the sand of the sea. And they went up on the breath of the earth, and compassed the camp of the saints around, and the beloved city; and fire came down from God out of heaven, and devoured them. And the devil that deceived them was cast into the Lake of Fire and brimstone, where the beast and false prophet are, and shall be tormented day and night for ever and ever. (Rev. 20:15)

"And whosoever was not found written in the Book of Life, was cast into the Lake of Fire."

Now, can you see some correlation or comparison of this to what we have been hearing about 2012? But everything that we are hearing is not biblical. Can this all be a coincidence? The ancient Mayas say December 21, 2012, is the end of an age, not the end of the earth. When the Tribulation starts, it will be the beginning of a new age—the 7-year Tribulation period that ends in the Battle of Armageddon. There are other sources saying seemingly the same thing, and none are biblical—a historian and a prophet in the 1500s, Nostradamus; The Hopi Indians; even a computer program called the Web-Bot Project. And more predictions, saying the same thing. Are they all a fluke? I know the Bible is truth, but what about all of the rest? But this you can say: There is an awful amount of agreement from totally unconnected sources. These sources weren't even on the same continent or from the same time period. These predictions aren't from some backwoods preacher in Tennessee, either. Some of these predictions are five hundred to over a thousand years old, and I am sure no one paid attention to any of it until now, or at least the last ten years, but because it is almost here, we are listening now. People are paying attention. We are now in 2010. The countdown has started!

# CHAPTER 4

## Creation

We have discussed some things about creation already, so we won't go back over that, but we get into new material regarding creation and the first family of humans. In Genesis 1:26 God said, *"Let us make man in our image."* And he did. He created us as a trinity also. He created us with a body, a soul, and a spirit—3 parts of us that work together as one. I am not in any way here talking about the Holy Trinity, but a different way of speaking about us. There is nothing holy about us, and I am first on that list. We are all sinners.

When God created Adam, he put him in the Garden of Eden to dress it and keep it (Gen. 2:15). "God created Adam out of the dust of the ground, and breathed life into him, and he became a living soul" (Gen. 2:7). God created everything out of the ground of the Earth, except Eve (Gen. 2:19). She was created from Adam (Gen. 2:21-23). "She was called Woman, because she was taken from the Man." But in the garden, God allowed someone else to be there, or he would have not been there. God is not a boundaryless God. The tempter was there also, he was allowed access . . .

Now the serpent was more subtle than any beast of the field which the Lord God hath made. And he said unto the woman, Yea, hath God said, Ye shall not eat of every tree of the garden? And the woman said unto the serpent, We may eat of the trees of the garden: But of the fruit of the tree which is in the midst of the garden, God hath said, *Ye shall not eat of it, neither shall ye touch it, lest ye die.* And the serpent said unto the woman, Ye shall not surely die: For God doth know that in the day ye eat thereof, then your eyes shall be opened, and ye shall be as gods, knowing good and evil. And when the woman saw the tree was good for food, and it was pleasant to the eyes and a tree to be desired to make one wise, she took of the fruit thereof, and did eat, and gave also unto her husband with her; and he did eat. And the eyes of both of them were opened, and they knew that they were naked; and they sewed fig leaves together, and made themselves aprons. (Gen. 3:1-7)

Adam and Eve were commanded not to eat of that tree, and that is exactly where they went. There was a 3-fold temptation of the woman: One, **Lust of the flesh**; two, **Lust of the eyes**; three, **Pride of life.** Genesis 3:6-7. Eve was tempted and seduced; she was deceived . . . Adam willfully straight-out sinned. The blame lies on Adam. He knew better . . . He plunged the earth into sin and chaos. His reasoning was not tainted by a sinful nature, like ours is. These 3 tactics the devil used to tempt Eve are the same 3 tactics he uses on mankind every day. Just think about it! These are the same 3 tactics the devil used on Christ in the wilderness. The 3 temptations of Christ (Matt. 4:3-11). The first Adam was weak and sinned, but Jesus Christ the second Adam was strong, and did not. I am sure Satan thought that his temptations, which worked the first time, would work again, but they did not. **Satan failed and was defeated!**

When God created Adam, God created him with age. Since the number of God is 3, because of the Holy Trinity, and God created man in their likeness, it comes across to me that Adam was created to be about 30 to 33 years old—a grown adult. I am sure Eve must have been the same. I am sure they were perfect in their creation. They were perfect in every way, except that they brought the curse of sin upon themselves and to all of humanity to follow them. They started the race of humanity, but it was started, flawed in sin! It became evident right from the first child born, Cain. He murdered his brother and became a murderer. The first child born to humanity, a murderer . . . thus our ancestry started with sin and murder. I can remember it being said at court trials of a person being tried for murder—that he had genetic flaws that caused him to have a predisposed weakness for murder. However, Cain's genetics was perfect. He had a sinful nature like all of us have. A murderer has the same sinful nature that we all have. We all have a sinful nature, which needs to be taken to the cross. Jesus Christ willingly went to that Roman cross and died for the Sins of Humanity at 3:00 p.m. AD 33. He became sin so we by faith can be free!

**For God so loved the world, that he gave his only begotten Son, that whosoever believeth in him should not perish, but have everlasting life. For God sent not his Son into the world to condemn the world; but the world through him might be saved. He that believeth on him is not condemned; but he that believeth not is condemned already, because he hath not believed in the name of the only begotten Son of God. (John 3:16-18)**

**This is the condemnation, that light is come into the world, and men loved darkness rather than light, because their deeds are evil. For everyone that doeth evil hateth the light, neither cometh to the light, lest his deeds should be reproved. But he that doeth truth cometh to the light, that his deeds may be made manifest, that they are wrought in God. (John 3:19-21)**

**Our Faith is that Jesus Christ, the Son of God, bled and died for our sins, and then on the 3rd day rose from the dead in newness of life. I believe that he died so I may live. Through his death for my sins I have eternal life.**

All the way back into ancient civilizations, blood offerings were used to appease their gods. The Mayas, the Aztecs, the Canaanites, ancient Chinese and Hebrews, all used animal, birds, and human beings for sin offerings and yearly offerings for their gods. They knew a life had to be taken, its blood spilled to appease their gods from anger. Our God is the same, that is why God allowed his only son to put aside his God head and come to earth, and become a human being. His main purpose in coming was to die for the sins of mankind once, for the past, present, and future

# CHAPTER 5

## The Flood

Lamach, the father of Noah, lived 777 years before he died, and Noah was 600 years old when the flood came (Gen. 7:6)

> Noah found grace in the eyes of the Lord. These are the generations of Noah: Noah was a just man and matured in his generations, and Noah walked with God. And Noah begat 3 sons, Shem, Ham, and Japheth. The earth was corrupt before God, and the earth was filled with violence. And God looked upon the earth, and behold it was corrupt; for all flesh had corrupted his way upon the earth. And God said to Noah, *The end of all flesh is come before me; for the earth is filled with violence through them; and, behold, I will destroy them with the earth.* (Gen. 6:8-13)

In Genesis 6:3, God made another announcement about humanity 120 years before the flood came: "*My spirit shall not always strive with man, for he also is flesh: yet his days shall be 120 years.*" When the flood came, everyone died, except Noah and his family and all of the animals in the ark. Christ also spoke about humanity just before the flood.

*But as the days of Noah were, so shall also the coming of the Son of man be. For as in the days that were before the flood they were eating and drinking, marrying and giving in marriage, until the day that Noah entered into the ark, and knew not until the flood came, and took them all away; so shall also the coming of the Son of man be.* (Matt. 24:37-39)

He will come, and very few people will be ready to meet him. Here is another passage from Genesis 6:5 to show the depraved nature of people before the flood, and you tell me if this doesn't sound like today: "And God saw the wickedness of man was great in the earth. And that every imagination of the thoughts of his heart was only evil continually." Now you tell me, isn't that the way it appears to be today? Corruption, violence, sexual sins, dishonesty, lack of compassion, pornography.

Noah's ark was a type of Jesus Christ. That huge wooden ark that took Noah and his sons over a hundred years to build became the savior of mankind, but another savior was coming, the Son of God. That ark rode the waves for 371 days with Noah and his family in it. 3 for God, and 7 for completion with God. Do you think God was furious at humanity back then? I think so . . . But he wasn't angry at everybody; the story of Noah's ark proves that. Do you think he is mad at humanity today? I believe so; however, he is not angry at everyone. God has children that love him all over the world. There are blood-bought believers all over the world now, anxiously waiting his Second Coming. We love him who first loved us!

It is very interesting to see the dimensions of the ark God gave to Noah. This was the size of the ark in biblical measurements. It was 300 cubits long, 50 cubits wide, 30 cubits high, and 3 stories high. Can you see God in all of these measurements? Look at the numbers! After the flood was over, God gave humanity the first rainbow. That rainbow had 7 colors in it, just like a rainbow has today. There were 7 colors for completion with God. It seems to me that God did not create humanity to live and practice tremendously violent, immoral evils like that—violence to children, the elderly, and the weak in society. It seems to me that if God didn't stop that, it wouldn't be fit for anyone to live at all. When a society or a civilization becomes depraved like that, it isn't fit for a decent man, woman, or child, or even an animal, to live in that. Many unbelievers feel that God is a nasty vindictive God, but I don't see him that way. If God doesn't intervene with the creation he had made, it would turn into total chaos, violence, and anarchy, unfit for a single godly person to exist. Everyone has choices. God gave us that freedom. People don't have to live depraved like that. They choose to do it. And they are responsible for their choices!

After God spoke to Noah (Gen. 7:4) before the flood, he told them to go into the ark and wait 7 days before the flood came. Another 7 was when the ark rested on Mt. Ararat in Turkey, in the 7th month. These numbers are another validation of God and his plan for mankind. **The numbers of God!**

However there is more to this story than what we see right here. Christ in his ministry refers to this very thing as he taught about his Second Coming or at the end of the age. It will come in two parts just like the flood came in two parts. Also the destruction of Sodom and Gomorrah came in two parts. Let me explain: After Noah and his sons finished building the Ark,"A type of Jesus Christ" or the savior of Godly humanity, God prompted animals to come from all over the earth to come and go into the Ark. After the animals were safely inside, he spoke to Noah and told him and his family to go into the Ark also. They went in and the door was sealed. However the Ark sat there on dry ground for 7 days before the rains came. But Noah and his family were safely inside. They were safe from the wrath to come. It seems to me this is how it will be at the Second Coming of Christ. We as believers will be raptured first to be safe with our Lord, then the Great Tribulation will start and end after 7 years with Christ coming back in great glory defeating the armies of Satan and the Anti-Christ and then preparing the earth for his one thousand year reign. The same happened with Sodom and Gomorrah, two angels took Lot and his family out first to safety, then destruction or the wrath of God came. God will do the same for us!

1st Thessalonians 4:15-18

"For this we say unto you by the word of the Lord, that we which are alive and remain unto the coming of the Lord shall not prevent them which are asleep. For the Lord himself will descend from heaven with a shout, with the voice of the archangel, and with the trump of God: and the dead in Christ shall rise first: Then we which are alive and remain shall be caught up together with them in the clouds to meet the Lord in the air: and so shall we ever be with the Lord. Wherefore comfort one another with these words.

1st Thessalonians 5:9

For God has not appointed us to wrath but to obtain salvation by our Lord Jesus Christ.

1st Corinthians 15:51-52

Behold I shew you a mystery; We shall not all sleep, but we shall be changed, In a moment in the twinkling of an eye, at the last trump: for the trumpet shall sound, and the dead shall be raised incorruptible, and we shall be changed.

Do you see that God does not appoint us to his wrath, no more then he did Noah and his family or Lot and his. He will take us out to be saved with him. Don't be deceived by prophesy teachers that teach there is no pre-tribulation Rapture. Now you know there is going to be one, and it is the very next thing to happen for the Blood-bought Believer and It could happen today . . . .

There is a lot of controversy about the flood as to when it happened and whether it indeed happened at all. But the Bible says it did, and I was taught to take the Bible literally; if it makes sense, seek no other sense. I believe all of the Word of God, not just bits and pieces, is true. When the book of Genesis in the Bible says there was a flood and talks about the details, I believe all that is written in God's Word is absolute truth. Man's reasoning isn't worth very much and that includes my own! However, there seems to be other evidences of Noah's Flood. In the last 50 years there have been reported sightings of it, by climbers of Mt. Ararat, which is seventeen thousand feet high, and there has also been satellite imagery. I don't know how much is fact, but there seems to be growing evidence. The thought of this gigantic wooden boat made of Cyprus wood being on top of that mountain is unbelievable! If not by the Flood, then how did it ever get up there, frozen in the ice for thousands of years?

There is also controversy as to when this happened and when it happened in relation to the creation of Adam. There are Bible historians and explorers that push creation back to ten thousand, even up to fourteen thousand years BC. I don't know why. 2 Peter 3:8 makes the comparison of *one day being compared to one thousand years and creation took 6 days.* The millennial reign of Christ is to be one thousand years as compared to the 7th day of the creation week, the day God rested. Why would there be a five-thousand-year span of time from the birth of Abraham to the end of the millennial reign of Christ, and then there be five thousand to eight thousand years before Abraham to the creation of Adam? It doesn't make biblical sense to me. If that is true, it makes God a god of disorder. God is not a god of disorder. There is now two thousand and ten years since the birth of Christ, and between the birth of Christ and the birth of Abraham two thousand years. There should be two thousand years between the birth of Abraham and the creation of Adam. Add this up and you will have approximately 6 thousand and ten years to this date today. Doesn't that make better sense biblically? Then the flood would have been between the time of Abraham and Adam.

# Chapter 6

## Abraham

Abraham grew up in Ur of the Chaldees. This was a wealthy, populous, pagan city in southern Mesopotamia. He was the son of Terah, who was not a godly man like his son Abram. Terah had 3 sons. He also was 70 years old when Abram was born. Abram grew up and married his half sister Sari, but she did not bear any children. In time, Abram's brother Haran, the father of Lot, died, and Terah, his father, decided to move to Haran, north of Canaan. "And Terah took Abram his son, and Lot the son of Haran, his grandson, and Sari his daughter-in-law, his son Abram's wife; and they went forth with them from Ur of the Chaldees, to go into the land of Canaan; and they came unto Haran, and dwelt there. And the days of Terah were two hundred and five years." It seems now the longevity of mankind is getting shorter.

When Abram was in Haran, God spoke to him and gave him a 3-fold journey.

> Now the Lord had said unto Abram, "*Get thee out of thy country, and from thy kindred, and from thy father's house, unto a land that I will show thee: and I will make of thee a great nation, and I will bless thee, and make thy name great; and thou shalt be a blessing: And I will bless them that bless*

*thee, and curse them that curseth thee: and in thee shall all the families of the earth be blessed."* (Gen. 12:1-3)

Here is a Divine promise from God about Abraham. God did not forget that promise to the present day. Just look at history and you can see it. Now back to Genesis 12:4-5:

> So Abram departed, as the Lord had spoken unto him; and Lot went with him: and Abram was seventy-five years old when he departed out of Haran. And Abram took Sari his wife, and Lot his brother's son, and all of their substance that they had gathered, and the souls they had gotten in Haran; and they went forth to go into the land of Canaan; and into the land of Canaan they came.

After Abram left Haran, he soon became rich in cattle, silver, and gold.

> And the Lord appeared unto Abram, and said, *"Unto thy seed will I give this land:"* and there built he an altar unto the Lord, who appeared unto him. (Gen. 12:7)

But Abram had no son to pass his lineage to, and he was already seventy-five years old. But God meant what he said to Abram; that land of Canaan would become, in time, Israel, the land of his people and the birthplace of his Son, Jesus Christ, and the birthplace of Abram's son Isaac. Jerusalem would be built there also, and it will, at the end of the millennial reign of Christ, become the site of the Holy City, The New Jerusalem, The City of God. The 3rd heaven will move down to planet Earth from where it is now.

> And I saw a new heaven and a new earth: for the first heaven and the first earth were passed away; and there was no more sea. And I John saw the holy city, the new Jerusalem, coming down from God out of

heaven, prepared as a bride adorned for her husband. And I heard a great voice out of heaven saying, quote: *Behold the tabernacle of God is with men, and he will dwell with them, and they shall be his people, and God himself shall be with them, and be their God. And God shall wipe away all tears from eyes; and there shall be no more death, neither sorrow or crying, neither shall there be any more pain: for the former things are passed away.* And he that sat upon the throne said, *"Behold, I make all things new."* And he said unto me, *"Write: for these words are true and faithful."* And he said unto me, *"It is done. I am the Alpha and the Omega, the beginning and the end. I will give unto him that is athirst of the fountain of the water of life freely. He that overcometh shall inherit all things and I will be his God and he shall be my son."* (Rev. 21:1-7)

If Abram had any idea how encompassing that promise was, he would have been dumbfounded! But Abram believed God by faith, as we must also, concerning the rich inheritance God has in store for us. I am sure if we could see what God has in store for us, it would dumbfound us as much as it did Abraham, for it is very hard for us to grasp the greatness of the Almighty, or the **Ways of God.**

Abram was in the land of Canaan many years and still did not have a son, and the Lord brought him forth abroad and said, *"Look now towards heaven, and tell the stars, if thou be able to number them:* and he said unto him, *So shall thy seed be."* And he, Abram, believed in the Lord; and he (God) counted it to him as righteousness (Gen. 15:5-6). Abram believed God by faith, just as we believe God by faith, and it will be counted to us, as righteousness. Abram had to wait until he was one hundred years old till his son Isaac was born. But he believed the promise, and through his seed the Savior of mankind, Christ the Lord, would be born.

God spoke to Abram again and said, "*Take me a heifer of 3 years old, and a she goat of 3 years old, and a ram of 3 years old, and a turtle dove and a young pigeon*" (Gen. 15:9), and Abram used these as a sacrifice unto the Lord. Numbers of God: 3.

And when Abram was ninety years old and nine, the Lord appeared to Abram, and said unto him, "*I am the Almighty God; walk before me and be thou perfect. And I will make my covenant between me and thee, and will multiply thee exceedingly.*" And Abram fell on his face: and God talked with him saying, "*As for me, my covenant is with thee, and thou shalt be a father of many nations. Neither shall thy name anymore be called Abram, but thy name shall be Abraham; for a father of many nations have I made thee. And I will make thee exceeding fruitful, and I will make nations of thee, and kings shall come out of thee. And I will establish my covenant between me and thee and thy seed after thee in their generations for an everlasting covenant, to be a God unto thee, and to thy seed after thee. And I will give unto thee, and to thy seed after thee, the land wherein thou art a stranger, all the land of Canaan, for an everlasting possession; and I will be their God.*" (Gen. 17:1-8)

And God said unto Abraham, "*As for Sari thy wife, thou shalt not call her name Sari, but Sarah shall be her name. And I will bless her, and give thee a son also of her: yea, I will bless her, and she shall be a mother of nations, kings of people shall be of her.*" (Gen. 17:15-16)

And the Lord appeared unto him [Abraham] in the plains of Mamre: and he sat in the tent door in the heat of the day; and he lifted up his eyes and looked, and lo, 3 men stood by him: and when he saw them, he ran to meet them from the tent door, and bowed himself toward the ground. (Gen. 18:1-2)

This was the Lord coming as an angel to announce the birth of their son Isaac. And also, the Lord told him while he was there, what he was going to do to Sodom. "And the Lord visited Sarah as he had said, and the Lord did unto Sarah as he had spoken. For Sarah conceived, and bare Abraham a son in his old age, at the set time of which God had spoken to him. And Abraham called the name of his son that was born unto him, whom Sarah bare to him, Isaac." (Gen. 21:1-3)

When the Lord appeared to Abraham in the plains of Mamre, he told Abraham what he was going to do to Sodom and Gomorrah, for the sin of that place was so great! God was going to destroy those two cities for the corruption, sexual sin, violence, and wickedness that was going on, and destroy them he did. Now the Lord said, *As it was in the days of Sodom and Gomorrah so shall it be at the second coming of the Son of Man.* It was evil just like it is now! Corruption and greed, dishonest, immoral political leaders and business leaders. Pornography, violence, rape, homosexuality, and child molestation are at epidemic levels, and spouses cheating on each other are everywhere. Narcissistic selfish people, who have no regard for anyone, are commonplace. There is total obsession about looks, sex, sex organs, and youth; divorce and broken families are the norm. People are so tattooed up it is scary. It is hard to even look at them. Very good economists and economics professors say capitalism as we know it is collapsing. We as a country are collapsing from the inside out, and most people are whistling away in denial. The debt levels of consumers have never been so high, but people flock to casinos, hoping to make a quick buck. Our governor has pushed for bigger and better casinos with more games to lose money at. Our state government wants more sports stadiums and bigger casinos, more ways to plunge people into financial ruin. We have sports athletes in our colleges on scholarships who read and write at a third-grade level. We have professional athletes who earn millions of dollars a year, doing something a society doesn't even need. And I recently read a survey that said within two years of retirement, 78 percent of these sports heroes are totally broke.

It is totally unbelievable. Where are we at, here? This whole recession or depression, whatever you want to call it, was caused, at least in my mind, by crooked bankers and corporate heads on steroids, for corruption. They trashed this country for evil gains. People already wealthy, who are full of insatiable greed . . . And this also includes companies and businesses that are owned and run by so-called Christian employers, or Christian businessmen, who are greedy, dishonest, and corrupt, and do terrible things to their employees and customers, and then sit in church on Sunday mornings and sing songs about the *Grace of God*. It is deplorable. When a country or nation would allow someone to defraud the public to the tune of fifty billion dollars and do it for decades and not be caught, that alone should tell all of us that something is wrong in Denmark. How this could get past the SEC all these years and not be caught or seen is absolutely unbelievable. All of these high-paid government inspectors and investigators couldn't see a thing (maybe they were too busy looking at Internet porn). And they even had whistle-blowers. This is a bad omen for our country, and these crooks make Ebenezer Scrooge look like the tooth fairy. But this is not only in politics and corporate banking, but in our churches as well. We have had decades of rich television preachers teach health and wealth doctrines while at the same time becoming multimillionaires at the expense of gullible, naive believers. There are television preachers that preach positive thinking and many ways to God. These teachers are false and lead people into more and more denial—denial as to where they really are. Maybe it would be like a money-hungry evangelist that held a tent revival outside of Sodom months before it was destroyed. He preached positive-thinking messages, and health and wealth doctrines; he taught everyone is beautiful in his or her own way. He preached feel-good sermons, and the offerings just kept rolling in. His book sales on positive living did so well; he came prancing out with expensive suits on with solid gold buttons on them. Wow! Was he the man or what? People flocked to the feel-good services and great rock and rap music and took home nothing. But everyone was entertained . . . and then the end came! Maybe that is where we are now.

Some senior very well-known economists say that since the creation of the Dow Jones Industrial Average around 1900 we have had 3 major economic cycles and that we have now peaked out of our very old supercycle, which goes back to early 1900s. They also say that the supercycle bubble has broken. We have seen the bubble in the stock indexes break, the real-estate bubble break, and now it seems that commodities and bonds will be the last shoe to drop. Now if we (United States) collapsed, would that necessarily mean the Second Coming of Christ would come? No, but we are the superpower of the world now, but probably not for long, and as we go, the rest of the world would follow, and that would set the stage for the Antichrist to step into power. Some economists even say 2012 could be a turning point. It seems to me that American capitalism has lost its way; we have lost our moral and ethical direction. I read an article in a financial journal that said today 1 percent of Americans own 90 percent of its wealth. That is like medieval Europe in the dark ages. Many people own homes but most are mortgaged so deeply, they owe more than what their home is worth. Homes have lost so much value in the last four or five years, home owners are underwater everywhere. That would mean that unless these home owners have large nest eggs, or retirements, they have a zero dollar net worth. Many less than zero. So the wealth of the middle class has moved to the superrich, as the middle class has moved down to the poor in many cases. The French Revolution started in 1789 because of economic hardship of commoners, under Louis XVI, and the French Revolution opened the door for Napoleon Bonaparte, who the forecaster Nostradamus says was the first Antichrist. By 1800, he was in power and tried to conquer Europe but failed. In the 1930s Adolf Hitler came to power in Germany, most probably because of the depression that Germany was in, and the world was in. Adolf Hitler tried to conquer western and eastern Europe and Russia. Nostradamus infers that he was the second Antichrist.

Hitler also was defeated. Now we are in a great economic crisis again. Maybe this one may be the worst of them all. It seems that the stage is being set for the third Antichrist, and this one is the real one, with an eye on the entire world—the leader of the **New World Order.**

# CHAPTER 7

# Jesus Christ: Birth and Childhood

Christ came from the root of David, who reigned in Israel for 33 years. The genealogy of Christ through his father Joseph is divided into 3 segments, which are divided into 14 generations each.

And in the 6th month the angel Gabriel was sent from God unto a city of Galilee, named Nazareth. To a virgin espoused to a man whose name was Joseph, of the house of David; and the virgin's name was Mary. And the angel came in unto her, and said, *"Hail, thou that are highly favored, the Lord is with thee: blessed art thou among women."* And when she saw him, she was troubled at his saying, and cast in her mind what manner of salutation this should be. And the angel said unto her, *"Fear not, Mary: for thou hast found favor with God. And, behold thou shalt conceive in thy womb, and bring forth a son, and shalt call his name JESUS. He shall be great, and shall be called the Son of the Highest: and the Lord God shall give unto him the throne of his father David: And he shall reign over the house of Jacob forever; and of his kingdom there shall be no end."* Then said Mary unto the angel, "How can this be, seeing I know not a man?" And the angel answered and said unto her, *"The Holy Ghost shall come upon thee and the power of the highest shall overshadow thee: therefore the holy thing which shall be born of thee shall be called the Son of God. And behold, thy cousin Elisabeth shall also conceive a son in her old age: and this is the 6th month with her, who was called barren. For with God nothing shall be impossible."* (Luke 1:26-37)

Did you notice the 6's in these passages? God did this for humanity, whose number is 6.

Mary arose in those days and went to visit her cousin Elisabeth, and she abode with Elisabeth for 3 months. Luke 1:39-56.

At the time of Christ's birth, when the angels appeared to the shepherds and announced that a savior was born, they gave him 3 titles: Savior, Messiah, and Lord (Yahweh). He was both God and man. After Christ was born in Bethlehem, there came wise men to Jerusalem, looking for the King of the Jews, for they saw his star in the east and came to worship him. Tradition says that there were 3 wise men and that they were kings, but that is not for sure. Also, an in-depth study into the Bethlehem Star has been done by Rick Larson, at www.bethlehemstar.net. It is a fascinating and enlightening investigation as to what the Star of Bethlehem actually was. Ancient star charts show what it was, and it is amazing how a configuration of planets, star clusters, and stars made up the Bethlehem Star and actually led the wise men west to Jerusalem and eventually to Bethlehem. The wise men were led to Christ, bearing 3 gifts fit for a king: (1) gold; (2) sweet-smelling frankincense, an expensive ingredient in the making of perfume; and (3) myrrh, a plant gum resin, sold as an expensive spice. There were 3 gifts, the number of God.

It was foreknown and foretold about Herod's attempt to kill the Christ child; he was Satan's man to destroy the child and stop the plan of God, for Satan would do anything to stop what was happening, even the **Slaughter of the Innocents**. But God knew what King Herod would do, inspired by the devil, and God had a plan to protect his Son. Since Mary and Joseph were poor, they had no finances to escape Herod's plan to kill the Christ child, but God was ready. He had already arranged in the heavens for a celestial arrangement of planets and stars to be seen by kings in the east. These wise men understood what they saw, got ready, and left for the trip of their lifetimes. Somehow they knew to bring 3 gifts for one king—rich gifts fit for a king, gifts that could finance the escape from Herod the infidel. As soon as the wise men finished worshipping the Christ child and left for home, an angel of the Lord appeared to Joseph and said, *"Arise take the young child and his mother and flee into Egypt, and stay there until I bring you word: for Herod will seek the young child to destroy him"* (Matt. 2:13). Now Joseph had the money to go, and he arose at night and took the young child and his mother and fled to Egypt, where they were safe. What a display of the greatness of God! Everything planned to the last detail.

> But when Herod was dead, behold an angel of the Lord appeared in a dream to Joseph in Egypt, saying, *"Arise, and take the young child and his mother and go into the land of Israel; for they are dead which sought the young child's life."* And he arose and took the young child and his mother, and came into the land of Israel. But when he heard that Archela'us did reign in Judea in the room of his father Herod, he was afraid to go thither: notwithstanding, being warned of God in a dream, he turned aside into parts of Galilee: And he came and dwelt in a city called Nazareth: that it might be fulfilled which was spoken by the prophets, "He shall be called a Nazarene." (Matt. 2:19-23)

Jesus grew up in the city of Nazareth, and very little is said in the Bible about his childhood, except that when he was 12 years old, he was taken to Jerusalem. When Joseph and Mary had fulfilled what they had come to Jerusalem to do, they, and the group they came with, returned and left for home, and they did not know that Jesus was not with them. They went a whole day's journey before they realized that. Realizing that he was not with them, Mary and Joseph returned to Jerusalem to find him.

> And it came to pass, after 3 days they found him in the temple, sitting in the midst of the doctors, both hearing them and asking them questions. And all that heard him were astonished at his understanding and his answers. (Luke 2:46)

# Chapter 8

# Ministry

Nothing more is said of Christ until he reached 30 years of age. We know his mother and father had more children. He had four stepbrothers and stepsisters.

> Is not this the carpenter's son? Is not his mother called Mary? And his brethren, James and Joses, and Simon, and Jude? And his sisters, are they not all with us? (Matt. 13:55-56)

So we see he had siblings, but what about his father? The Gospels say almost nothing about his father Joseph, but it seems he must have been a very godly man. It also seems that he must have died sometime in Jesus's early years, but more than that, nothing else is said about Christ's life before the start of his ministry. His ministry started after he was baptized by John the Baptist. He was 30 years of age (Luke 3:22-23). "After Jesus was baptized and he was full of the Holy Ghost, he was led by the spirit into the wilderness for forty days where he was tempted of the devil" (Luke 4:1-13). He was tempted by the devil in the wilderness 3 times. Why only 3 times? It was the same temptations that were used on Adam and Eve. **Adam failed; Christ didn't!**

And the 3rd day there was a marriage in Cana of Galilee; and the mother of Jesus was there. And both Jesus and his disciples were called to the marriage. And when they wanted wine, the mother of Jesus said unto him, "They have no wine." Jesus said unto her, *"Woman, what have I to do with thee? Mine hour is not yet come."* His mother said unto the servants, "Whatsoever he says unto you, do it." And there was set there 6 waterpots of stone, after the manner of the purifying of the Jews, containing two or three firkins apiece. Jesus said unto them, *"Fill the waterpots with water,"* and they filled them up to the brim. And he said unto them, *"Draw out now and bear unto the governor of the feast."* And they bear it. When the ruler of the feast had tasted the water that was made wine, and knew not whence it was, (but the servants which drew the water knew,) the governor of the feast called the bridegroom, and said unto him, "Every man at the beginning sets forth good wine; and when all have well drunk, then that, which is worse; but you have kept the good wine until now." This was the beginning of the miracles that Jesus did in Cana of Galilee and manifested forth his glory; and his disciples believed on him. (John 2:1-11)

Cana of Galilee is very close to the 33rd parallel northern latitude. Do you notice the 3's and the number 6 for humanity in these passages? Even the location where this happened. The 3's are for God.

*In the beginning was the Word, and the Word was with God, the Word was God. The same was in the beginning with God. All things were made by him; and without him was not anything made that was made. And the light shined in darkness; and the darkness comprehended it not. There was a man sent from God, whose name was John. The same came for a witness, to bear witness of the Light, that all men through him might believe. He was not that Light, but was sent to bear witness of that Light. That was the true Light, which lighteth every man that comes into the world. He was in the world, and the world was made by him, and the world knew him not. He came unto his own, and his own received him not. But as many as received him, to them gave the power to become the sons of God, even to them that believe on his name: Which were born not of blood, nor of the will of the flesh, nor of the will of man, but of God. And the Word was made flesh, and dwelt among us, (and we beheld his glory, the glory as of the only begotten of the Father,) full of grace and truth.* (John 1:1-14)

What a word picture of Jesus Christ! That word picture shows us exactly who and what he really is and was. Notice how he was described: (1) **He was the light of mankind. (2) He was full of grace. (3) He was full of truth. He was God the Creator! That became a human being on planet Earth.**

Jesus said of himself, *"Destroy this temple and in 3 days I will raise it up"* (John 2:19). Another incident was when Jesus spoke to the Samaritan woman at the well. It was about the 6th hour, the number of humanity. Yet another incident, another number. "After spending time in Samaria the Lord went back to Cana of Galilee and healed a nobleman's son. The fever left the boy on the 7th hour" (John 4:52). Jesus spoke of himself. *"I am the way, the truth and the life, no man comes to the father, but by me"* (John 14:6). Notice again the 3 ways the Lord spoke of himself. He totally explained here who he was. He is the only way to eternal life. There is no other way to heaven or to God, but by Jesus Christ and what he did on the cross. The life giver died for the sins of humanity; he shed his blood for our sins and died for us. He became the Lamb of God, was slain for our iniquity, and became the sin offering so we may have eternal life, not damnation of hell with the devil and his fallen angels. We can be saved by faith from this, but not Satan and his angel legions, for Christ did not die for them. There was no bloodshed for them, but it was for us. There is no hope for them, for very shortly they will be cast into the lake of fire, which will burn them forever. But not for blood-bought believers. Jesus Christ made a way out for us.

Nearing the end of Christ's 3-year-long ministry, his friend Lazarus, the brother of Martha and Mary, became sick. Jesus loved these 3 people, and when he heard that Lazarus was sick, he waited where he was for two days. "When Jesus heard that Lazarus was sick, he said, *'This sickness is not unto death, but for the glory of God, that the Son of God might be glorified thereby'*" (John 11:4). Then the Lord and his disciples left where they were and went to Judea.

> Again Martha speaking, "Yea Lord: I believe that though art the Christ: but Mary sat still in the house. Then said Martha unto Jesus, "Lord, if you would have been here my brother would not have died. But I know that even now, whatsoever you will ask of God, God will give it to you." Jesus said unto her, *"Thy brother shall rise again."* Martha said unto him, "I know that he shall rise again in the resurrection at the last day." Jesus said unto her, *"I am the resurrection and the life: he that believeth in me, though he were dead, yet shall he live: and whosoever lives and believes in me shall never die. Believest thou this?"* (John 11:20-26)

Did you notice how the Lord addressed himself again? As **I AM.**

> Again Martha speaking, "Yea Lord: I believe that though art the Christ, the son of God, which should come into this world." And when she had so said, she went her way, and called her sister Mary secretly, saying, "The Master

has come, and calleth for you." And as soon as she heard that, she arose quickly and came unto him. Now Jesus was not yet come into the town, but was in the place where Martha met him. (John 11:27-30)

When the Lord came to the place where Lazarus was, he cried with a loud voice, *"Lazarus come forth"* (John 11:43).

And he that was dead came forth, bound hand and foot with grave clothes; and his face was bound about with a napkin. Jesus said unto them, *"Loose him and let him go."* (John 11:44)

Now the Lord waited 4 days to resurrect Lazarus, after he died. Why? Do you think he didn't want the resurrection of Lazarus to be confused with his own resurrection in 3 days? I believe so. 3 is the number of God. He was God in the flesh—the Creator!

Then Jesus 6 days before the Passover came to Bethany, where Lazarus was which had been dead, whom he raised from the dead. There they made him a supper; and Martha served: but Lazarus was one of them that sat at the table with him. Then took Mary a pound of ointment of spikenard, very costly, and anointed the feet of Jesus, and wiped his feet with her hair: and the house was filled with the odor of the ointment. Then said one of his disciples, Judas Iscariot, Simon's son, which should betray him, Why was not this ointment sold for 300 pence and given to the poor? This he said, not that he cared for the poor; but because he was a thief, and had the bag, and knew what was put therein. Then said Jesus, *"Let her alone: against the day of my burying hath she kept this. For the poor you always have with you; but me you will not always have."* (John 12:1-8)

Notice the 300 pence—it is the number 3 again. Also notice 6 days before the Passover—the Passover for humanity. The Lord also knew that Judas was a thief, and he allowed him to carry their money anyway.

> In two days was the feast of the Passover, and of unleavened bread: [notice this was four days later than the supper that Mary, Martha, and Lazarus had for the Lord] the chief priests and the scribes sought how they might take him by craft, and put him to death. But they said Not on a feast day, lest there be an uproar of the people. And being in Bethany in the house of Simon the leper, as he sat at meat, there came a woman having an alabaster box of ointment of spikenard very precious; and she broke the box and poured it on his head. And there were some that had indignation within themselves, and said, "Why was this waste of ointment made? For it might have been sold for more than 300 pence, [notice 300 pence again] and been given to the poor," and they murmured against her. And Jesus said, *"Let her alone; why trouble her? She has wrought a good work on me. For you have the poor with you always, and whensoever you will you may do them good: but me you will have not always. She has done what she could: she has come aforehand to anoint my body for the burying. Verily I say unto you, Wheresoever this gospel shall be preached throughout the whole world, this also that she has done shall be spoken of as a memorial of her."* (Mark 14:1-10)

And Judas Iscariot, one of his 12 disciples, went unto the chief priests to betray him. Seems like all of this money that the insincere, greedy, crook Judas saw being spent on the Lord was just too much for him. He had to do something about this immediately.

And when they [scribes] heard it, they were glad, and promised to give HIM money. And he [Judas] sought how he might conveniently betray him. (Mark 14:11)

The price of the betrayal: 30 pieces of silver. Look at the 3's again. Historians say this might have been between twelve to fifteen thousand dollars in our money.

# CHAPTER 9

## Crucifixion and Resurrection

After the Last Supper in the upper room was over, they all left and went into the mount of Olives. And they came to a place called Gethsemane: and he said to his disciples, "Sit here while I go to pray." And he took with him (1) Peter and (2) James and (3) John, and began to be sore amazed, and to be very heavy. And he said unto them, *"My soul is exceeding sorrowful unto death: tarry ye here and watch."* And he went forward a little, and fell on the ground and prayed that, if it were possible, the hour might pass from him. And he said, *"Abba, Father, all things are possible for you; take this cup from me: nevertheless not what I will, but what you wilt."* And he came and found them sleeping, and said unto Peter, Simon, *"Sleepest thou? Could you not watch one hour? Watch and pray, lest you enter into temptation. The spirit truly is ready, but the flesh is weak."* And again he went away, and prayed, and spoke the same words. And when he returned, he found them asleep again, (for their eyes were heavy) and they had no idea what to answer him. And he came the 3rd time and said unto them, *"Sleep on now, and take your rest: it is enough, the HOUR has come;*

*behold the Son of man is betrayed into the hands of sinners."*
(Mark 14:32-41)

Almost immediately after, the Lord was arrested and taken to be tried by the chief priests and the Sanhedrin. The nightmare he dreaded had started. He would be tried in that terrible night 3 times by 3 different people: Caiphas, Pilate, and Herod. He was mocked, beat, spit upon, and whipped until he was almost unrecognizable as a human being. His day of terror was here, and he faced it head-on. But as the Lord faced unbelievable abuse inside, outside Peter denied his Lord 3 times. He must have been very afraid. But he showed more bravery than the others, for they ran away and hid. The Lord stood alone.

By 9:00 a.m. (our time; their time, the 3rd hour), the Lord had carried the cross out of town to the place of his crucifixion, and was crucified. He was suspended between heaven and earth. He must have been in so much pain, physical and emotional; he would have blacked out if he wasn't such a strong person. But he knew he was dying for all of humanity, past, present, and future. As the Gospel song says, *"For when he was on the cross, I was on his mind,"* he died for us in the future, as well as saints of God who died in the ancient past. He died for the animals that crucified him. He suffered and died that day, so all of humanity might be saved. He was not only the God of all peoples but the God of the individual. He is the God of each one of his children. We can go to God and say, "Abba, Father, Dad . . ." ***Oh, what a Savior!***

Now many historians believe that Christ was crucified on April 3, AD 33. He was 33 years old. His ministry lasted 3 years. His ministry was centered mostly in Galilee, Samaria and Judea, whose location on the globe is crossed by the 33rd parallel, northern latitude. Mesopotamia, the fertile crescent where civilization and humanity began, is also crossed by the 33rd parallel. Christ's ministry started at Cana of Galilee, which is close to the 33rd parallel. Also, Megiddo, where the Battle of Armageddon is to be fought, lies almost directly on the 33rd parallel. Coincidence? What do you think?

When the Lord was crucified, there were a total of 3 crosses there. Also, 3 spikes were driven into his hands and feet. "And when the 6th hour was come [12:00 p.m. our time], there was darkness over the whole land until the 9th hour [3:00 p.m. our time today]" (Mark 15:33). The Lord hung on the cross 6 hours divided by 2 spans of 3 hours. 6 for humanity; the 3's are for God. He died on the ninth hour. A sign that said, **"King of the Jews,"** was nailed to the top of his cross. It was written 3 times in 3 different languages: Hebrew, Greek, and Latin. Also when Christ was dying on the cross, he made 7 statements, and the last statement, he cried with a loud voice, *"It is finished!"* and he died. He finished what he came to do! He who was the Creator, the Life, and the Light of the world died that day! When the moon came up that night in Judea, there was a bloody eclipse. The moon was going into eclipse on the other side of the world at 3:00 p.m. when the Lord died . . . Hours later it was seen by the Judeans, a full moon in blood red. It stuns you to think about it . . . Everything was timed to the very hour! It is beyond our comprehension! No wonder he said, *"Father forgive them, for they know not what they do."*

> And Jesus cried with a loud voice, and gave up the ghost. And the veil of the temple was rent in twain from the top to the bottom. And when the centurion, which stood over against him, saw that he so cried out, and gave up the ghost and expired, he said, "Truly this man was the son of God." (Mark 15:37-39)

The veil of the temple being torn from top to bottom was the physical show that a new dispensation started on that day: the Age of Grace. Christ fulfilled the Law of Moses, so we do not live under the Old Testament Law anymore. It is too bad that so many so-called Christian churches and denominations, Christian groups, and even cults do not understand that. They are still back in the old Hebrew Law and works of the Law. How foolish! We now live by Faith in the Grace of God, believing what Christ did that day for us on that Roman cross. We are saved by Faith ONLY, not by works, or doing church traditions, or doing religious things; no one has ever been saved by any of that. Not by how many times you go to church services, or how much money you put in the offering plate, or how many doors you knocked on, or how many times you cleaned the church, or how many candles you lit, or how many times you have gone to mass, or how much religious clothing or religious jewelry that you wear, but only by Faith, believing that Christ died for your sins on the cross that day. And that he rose from the dead on the 3rd day. Many days later, after meeting with his disciples and believers, he rose to heaven and is now seated at the right hand of the Father. **He totally completed what he came to do**.

After the Lord rose from the dead, he asked Peter 3 times, if he loved him. (John 21:15)

# CHAPTER 10

## More Things about Number 3

1. There are 66 books in the Bible.
2. There are 3 primary colors, which form all colors that we look at every day.
3. Atoms have 3 particles:
    1. Protons
    2. Electrons
    3. Neutrons
4. There are 3 basic chemical reaction substances:
    1. Acids
    2. Bases
    3. Salts
5. When Christ described the Holy Spirit, he said he would reprove the world of 3 things:
    1. Sin
    2. Righteousness
    3. Judgment
6. Animals were created to live in 3 areas:
    1. Land
    2. Water
    3. Air

7. Water, one of mankind's essential elements, is composed of 3 parts:
    1. 1 part hydrogen
    2. 2 parts oxygen
8. Food has 3 main parts that provide energy:
    1. Protein
    2. Fat
    3. Carbohydrates
9. There are 3 states of matter:
    1. Solid
    2. Liquid
    3. Gas
10. A solid has 3 dimensions
    1. Length
    2. Width/breadth
    3. Height
11. There are 3 virtues:
    1. Faith
    2. Hope
    3. Love
12. Dimensions of space:
    1. Up/down
    2. Left/right
    3. Forward/backward
13. The sum of human capability:
    1. Thought
    2. Word
    3. Deed
14. Mankind's 3 greatest enemies:
    1. The world
    2. The flesh
    3. The devil
15. Chromosomes are in 3 types of patterns.

16. Although numbers and statistics may vary, it seems that there are 6.6 or 6.7 billion people living on planet Earth right now.
17. A circle = 360 degrees, 3 for God, 6 for mankind.
18. The air we breathe has the following composition:
    1. 78 percent nitrogen
    2. 21 percent oxygen
    3. 1 percent carbon dioxide

# CHAPTER 11

## Conclusion

Now you can see, as I have, that everything about us has to do with God—from creation to our time in history. The numbers of God also show this, especially number 3, the number of God. From the air we breathe, to the water we drink, the food we eat, and where we are located in the cosmos. **It is all God.** God is the glue that holds molecules and atoms together to make mass. He is the substance that holds Galaxies in place. He is the dark energy, the black holes in deep space. He is the creator of stars and planets, and that same God, Jesus Christ, one of the 3 came into this world and became a human being to die for our sin, so we have a way out and be saved from the wrath to come. Through him we may have eternal life if we accept him by faith. If you do not know him as your Savior, today can be your day to change that. The numbers show it. Ever since Satan brought sin into the Cosmos, God had a plan how to deal with it and him. And we as humanity became part of that plan. God will end it, with sin being erased from the Cosmos again. And we who are blood-bought believers will be there to see it. And we will live to spend eternity in glory with our God.

www.ingramcontent.com/pod-product-compliance
Lightning Source LLC
Chambersburg PA
CBHW020405290526
45785CB00005B/2442